P9-CSU-642

The Secret World of

KABBALAH

7he Secret WOrld of
KABBALAH

Judith Z. Abrams

KAR-BEN
PUBLISHING

Coweta County Public Library System
85 Literary Lane
Newnan, GA 30265

Copyright © 2006

All U.S. rights reserved. No part of this book may be reproduced, stored in a retrieval system, or transmitted in any form or by any means—electronic, mechanical, photocopying, recording, or otherwise—without the prior written permission of Kar-Ben Publishing, Inc., except for the inclusion of brief quotations in an acknowledged review.

Kar-Ben Publishing, Inc.
A division of Lerner Publishing Group
241 First Avenue North
Minneapolis, MN 55401 U.S.A.

Website address: www.karben.com

Library of Congress Cataloging-in-Publication Data

Abrams, Judith Z.
      The secret world of kabbalah / by Judith Z. Abrams.
         p.   cm.
      ISBN-13: 978–1–58013–224–4 (pbk. : alk. paper)
      ISBN-10: 1–58013–224–3 (pbk. : alk. paper)
         1. Cabala—History—Juvenile literature. 2. Mysticism—Judaism—Juvenile literature.
      I. Title.
      BM526.A26 2006
      296.1'6—dc22   2005022606

Manufactured in the United States of America
1 2 3 4 5 6 – BP – 11 10 09 08 07 06

Dedicated, in great gratitude

To:
Everton A. Edmondson, M.D.
For Strength of Body

To:
Bill, Glenn, John, Lon, and Reed Lowenstein
For Strength of Spirit

Contents

What Is Kabbalah?

*K*abbalah has become fashionable . . . at least a certain sort of
kabbalah has become fashionable.
It is important for people to know
some basic concepts in Jewish
mysticism, so they can distinguish
the true essence of Jewish mysticism from what is just fashionable.

> While the word
> kabbalah has many
> meanings, in this book
> we'll define it as
> "hidden wisdom."

Kabbalah is derived from the Hebrew verb *kibbel* which means
"to receive." Just as the *Tanach* (the Hebrew name for the Bible)
and Rabbinic Literature (e.g., the *Talmud*) have been passed
down, so a third body of knowledge, a hidden knowledge know
as kabbalah, has come down to us through the ages. So while the
word kabbalah has many meanings, in this book we'll define it as
"hidden wisdom."

Any discussion of kabbalah involves talking about God. God is, by
definition, infinite and cannot accurately be described in human
language. Therefore, we'll be using analogies in this book to help us

describe what cannot accurately be described in words and to think about things that are infinite, limited by our finite minds.

The Journey

*L*et's think of kabbalah as a journey. We can liken our journey to climbing to the summit of Mount Everest, the tallest mountain in the world. The top of Mount Everest is as high up in the atmosphere as an airplane is at its usual cruising altitude: about 30,000 feet.

Now, if you think about those safety demonstrations they always do before a plane takes off, you'll recall that they tell you that if the cabin loses air pressure, an oxygen mask will drop down, and you should put it on to breathe. This is because at any height above 25,000 feet there is not enough oxygen in the air to sustain human life. The higher you go into the atmosphere, the less oxygen and warmth there is to sustain life.

If you were taken right now from wherever you are and transported to the top of Mount Everest, you would be unconscious in thirty seconds and dead in two minutes. It is only through careful training, good judgment, and the supervision of an expert guide that anyone is able to reach the summit of Mount Everest and return safely.

Many people have died in their quest to conquer Mount Everest. Most of them die after they have reached the top. They often suffer from something called Summit Fever. When they are being consumed by Summit Fever, all they can think about is reaching the top of the world. Then, after they have reached the summit, with their strength and concentration spent, they often make mistakes on their way down. These mistakes, made so high up in the atmosphere, without easy access to rescue, can prove fatal.

Why am I telling you all this? Because kabbalah is the journey to come as closely in touch with God as you can. It involves extreme concentration. You may be tempted to discard things that might distract you, such as talking, sleeping, or even eating, as you push toward your goal.

The quest to reach God is just as dangerous as trying to reach the top of Mount Everest. You need a good guide, one who's already been to the top, to help you up the mountain. You need a guide who can tell when you're letting Summit Fever cloud your judgment, one who can turn you around and get you back down safely before you make a very serious mistake that could cause you harm.

This is why kabbalah has traditionally been taught one-on-one. Each person needs a guide s/he will trust and obey in order to make the climb safely. Each person is different and has different needs. Kabbalah is definitely not "one-size-fits-all."

There is another lesson to be learned from this analogy about climbing Mount Everest. The summit, the goal, is the same for everyone. There are, however, many ways to reach that goal, and the climbs are very, very different.

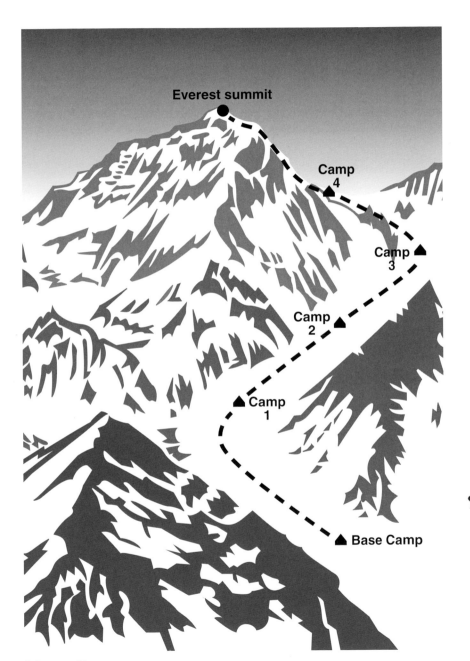

MOUNT EVEREST SEEN FROM THE SOUTHERN SIDE, SHOWING THE STANDARD ROUTE

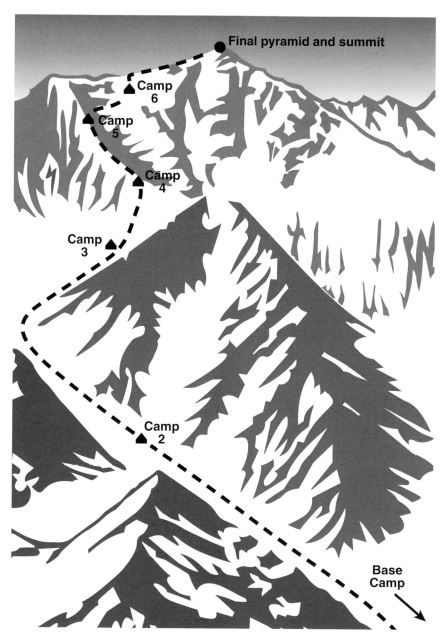

MOUNT EVEREST SEEN FROM THE NORTHERN SIDE, SHOWING THE
NORTHERN ROUTE WITH CAMPS

For example, when one approaches Mount Everest from the south, one has to hike on foot for two weeks before one even reaches Base Camp at around 17,000 feet. From there, four camps are set up and climbers must move through an ice fall—a perilous shifting mass of enormous ice blocks— something like a waterfall of giant ice cubes the size of large buildings.

If you really want to make this journey, you'll have to stick with the path you've chosen until you reach the top.

One can also approach Mount Everest from the north side. From this side, one can actually drive to Base Camp. From Base Camp there are six camps on the way to the top. It is a much more difficult climb to make, even though there is no ice fall to climb through from that direction.

Why is this important? Because all religions have their own forms of kabbalah. Each has its own ways of connecting with God in the most complete way possible.

Some people say, "Well, all religions are alike . . . they all teach the same things in the end." This is true: the higher you go, and the more you know about God, the more similar religions seem.

But here's the rub: if you really want to reach the summit of Mount Everest, you have to choose a path and stick to it. You can't say, "I'll do the south side this week and the north side next week and the east side the week after that." You'd end up spending all your time circling around the bottom of the mountain.

Similarly, you can't say, "I'll try the Jewish route to God this week and the Buddhist way the next week and the Muslim way the week after that." If you really want to make this journey, you'll have to stick with the path you've chosen until you reach the top. There, you'll be able to meet other people who have chosen different routes to get to the same place.

The Choice Is Yours

*W*hat if you don't want to make the journey to cultivate a close relationship with God but still want to know more about kabbalah?

Let's return to our analogy. While I love reading about Mount Everest, I would never be able to reach Base Camp. Just going to the mountains of New Mexico gave me an altitude-induced headache. But reading about Mount Everest still gives me a thrill.

If you don't believe in God, or if you believe in God but don't want to cultivate a close relationship with God, you can still enjoy learning about kabbalah. It's like the difference between climbing the mountain and reading or watching a movie about it. Just reading about kabbalah can help expand your intellectual and emotional horizons, even if you don't connect with God spiritually.

> Just reading about kabbalah can help expand your intellectual and emotional horizons, even if you don't connect with God spiritually.

Hiding In Plain Sight

*S*tudying kabbalah requires you to live comfortably with things that seem to be contradictions. One of these contradictions is the idea that some of kabbalah (in fact, a lot of it!) is hiding in plain sight. What does that mean? Perhaps it can best be explained by a story.

> **Studying kabbalah requires you to live comfortably with things that seem to be contradictions.**

*O*nce there was a boy who lived far out in the country. One day he told his parents, "I want to go see the king." So they gave him some food, put him on a horse, and sent him on his way. The journey was pleasant. The sun shone, the gentle rolling hills were filled with fields and flowers. Finally, the boy came to the very farthest outpost of the king's domain. There, an old gatekeeper congratulated him on reaching this point.

The boy spent several pleasant days with the old man telling him about his journey, but then a nagging thought arose in the back of his mind. "This is nice . . . but I'm not with the king." So, thanking the gatekeeper for his hospitality, he set back out toward the palace.

Now the going wasn't so easy. The terrain was rough and the weather was rainy and cold. For many a day and night, the boy and his horse had to survive on the smallest of rations. At long last, they reached the next fence around the king's domain. The boy was greeted as a hero.

"How brave and talented you are to have made it to this point!" the people proclaimed. "You deserve a parade, money, and every earthly wish you could desire."

Well, how could the boy turn that down? He stayed there quite some time, enjoying all these rewards for his bravery. After a while, though, that same nagging thought recurred. "This is nice . . . but I'm still not with the king." The people warned him that the road ahead was dangerous, but the boy could not be dissuaded.

Now the terrain was so rugged that he had to leave his horse behind. He had to survive on bugs, leaves, and wild berries. As he crawled up and down rocky mountains, sleet, hail, and ever-dark skies hovered over him. At long last, he reached the next gate of the king's domain. There, the boy was praised not only for his physical courage but for his moral courage as well. The people revered him as a great spiritual teacher and asked him to stay and teach them all the lessons that his journey had taught him.

So while he rested and nursed his wounds, people came from near and far to learn from him. And even though this was exalted work, after a while he couldn't help thinking, "This is nice, but I'm still not with the king." So he set out, prepared for even worse hardships than he had endured before.

He became a beggar, shoeless, in rags. He thought only of his pilgrim-

age to see the king. Whether he lived or died became inconsequential to him. He walked on, through freezing cold and blazing heat. At long last, he came to the king's palace. He opened the door, expecting to see a glorious hall, gorgeously dressed courtiers, and, of course, the king in all his glory. That's not what he saw. He saw himself, in his old house, setting out to meet the king. This self, healthy and still young, greeted the dirty, barefoot beggar. The boy did not know what to make of this vision. "Am I dreaming? Am I dead?" he asked.

"No," said his old self.

"Then where is the king?"

"Have you not guessed? You have always been with the king."

"Was the journey then in vain?" he cried in sorrow. "Was all that I suffered a waste?"

"Yes and no," said the boy, who was the king, who was himself. "As long as you thought the king was 'out there' you would never be able to see that the king was really 'in here,'" said the boy, gently touching the beggar's chest.

Α nd with that, the boy was transported back to his home, with all his wounds healed, restored to wholeness in every way. And from that day onward, he lived in joy . . . but also with care, knowing that he was always in the presence of the king.

The boy could only grasp this great insight after making an exhausting trip and undergoing numerous hardships. We are much the same way. We are with God all the time. God's presence and wisdom are very easy to detect—hiding in plain sight—just the way the king's presence was always with the boy.

The Tanach Is A Mystical Text

*T*he most important mystical text is one you already know—the Tanach, the acronym of the first letters *(taf, nun, chaf)* of the three sections of the Hebrew Bible: *Taf* stands for Torah (Five Books of Moses), *Nun* for *Nevi'im* (Prophets) and *Chaf* for *Ketuvim* (Writings). The Tanach is full of concepts that lay the foundation for the rest of Jewish mysticism.

The very first chapter of the Torah is one of Judaism's important mystical texts. It contains the first story of creation. In this account, there are no trees of knowledge, talking snakes, or fig leaves. This story describes the orderly creation of the world. First God creates "containers": 1) heaven, 2) water and air, and 3) earth. Then God fills each container with its proper contents: 1) sun, moon, and stars in the heavens, 2) sea creatures and birds in the water and air, and 3) animals and human beings on the earth. On the seventh day, God rests, creating Shabbat.

Let's look at the acccount of the first day of creation. You'll need to count Hebrew letters for this exercise. Here are the first five sentences of the Bible:

1 בְּרֵאשִׁית בָּרָא אֱלֹהִים אֵת הַשָּׁמַיִם וְאֵת הָאָרֶץ :

2 וְהָאָרֶץ הָיְתָה תֹהוּ וָבֹהוּ וְחֹשֶׁךְ עַל־פְּנֵי תְהוֹם
וְרוּחַ אֱלֹהִים מְרַחֶפֶת עַל־פְּנֵי הַמָּיִם :

3 וַיֹּאמֶר אֱלֹהִים יְהִי **אוֹר** וַיְהִי־**אוֹר** :

4 וַיַּרְא אֱלֹהִים אֶת־הָ**אוֹר** כִּי־טוֹב וַיַּבְדֵּל אֱלֹהִים
בֵּין הָ**אוֹר** וּבֵין הַחֹשֶׁךְ :

5 וַיִּקְרָא אֱלֹהִים לָ**אוֹר** יוֹם וְלַחֹשֶׁךְ קָרָא לָיְלָה
וַיְהִי־עֶרֶב וַיְהִי־בֹקֶר יוֹם אֶחָד

*When God began creating the heavens and the earth, the earth was dark and disorganized and dimness was on the face of the deep and God's spirit hovered on the surface of the waters. And God said, "Let there be **light**." And there was **light**. And God saw that the **light** was good and God made a difference between the **light** and the darkness. And God called the **light** "Day" and called the dark "Night" and there was evening and there was morning, the first day. (Genesis 1:1-5)*

24

As a warm up, count how many Hebrew words there are in the first sentence. (Words connected by hyphens count as two words.) Now count how many Hebrew words there are in the second sentence.

Seven is a number you see frequently in Jewish mysticism.

You should have found seven words in the first sentence and fourteen in the second sentence. Seven is a number you see frequently in Jewish mysticism: seven days in a week, seven branches on

SEAL OF STATE OF ISRAEL

the menorah in the Temple, seven known planets at that time, seven years in the ancient agricultural cycle.

Now count how many letters are in the first sentence. Can you see the connection between 7, 14 and 28?

In the Torah, what's in the middle of a sentence is the most important thing. The middle word of the first sentence in the Torah is the two-letter word made up of the letters *alef* and *taf,* the first and last letters of the Hebrew alphabet. So the most important word of the first sentence in the whole Torah encompasses everything "from A to Z." It's also a word that can't be translated.

2 5

Et means that what follows (heaven and earth) is the direct object of the preceding verb (create). So it really signifies a direction. Such momentum, which can't be encompassed in human words, is the most important thing in moving toward God's creation of the universe.

Now count how many times the word *or,* (light) occurs in this passage. You should come up with five. You'll see a little later why that's important. Just remember that this light comes *before* the stars, sun, or moon were created, so this is a different sort of light than that given off by heavenly bodies.

Like so much else in Jewish mysticism, this level of text study can be distorted. Some people claim that there are codes in the Torah that can predict the future, and they may offer to sell them to you. A good rule of thumb is this: if someone's trying to sell you something, be it merchandise or a certain religious or political point of view, then they're not likely to be a genuine teacher of kabbalah and you should be wary of them.

Now, remember that we counted the number of times the word "light" occurred in the account of the first day of creation. Do you recall the story where Moses sees a bush that's burning but not burning up? The word used for bush there is *sneh,* and it's only used in the story of the burning bush and one other place in Torah, so it's a very rare word. Count the number of times the word *sneh* shows up in this passage about the burning bush:

26

וּמֹשֶׁה הָיָה רֹעֶה אֶת־צֹאן יִתְרוֹ חֹתְנוֹ כֹּהֵן מִדְיָן 1
וַיִּנְהַג אֶת־הַצֹּאן אַחַר הַמִּדְבָּר וַיָּבֹא אֶל־הַר
הָאֱלֹהִים חֹרֵבָה :
וַיֵּרָא מַלְאַךְ יְהוָה אֵלָיו בְּלַבַּת־אֵשׁ מִתּוֹךְ 2
הַסְּנֶה וַיַּרְא וְהִנֵּה הַסְּנֶה בֹּעֵר בָּאֵשׁ וְהַסְּנֶה
אֵינֶנּוּ אֻכָּל :
וַיֹּאמֶר מֹשֶׁה אָסֻרָה־נָּא וְאֶרְאֶה אֶת־הַמַּרְאֶה 3
הַגָּדֹל הַזֶּה מַדּוּעַ לֹא־יִבְעַר הַסְּנֶה :
וַיַּרְא יְהוָה כִּי סָר לִרְאוֹת וַיִּקְרָא אֵלָיו אֱלֹהִים 4
מִתּוֹךְ הַסְּנֶה וַיֹּאמֶר מֹשֶׁה מֹשֶׁה וַיֹּאמֶר הִנֵּנִי :

*Moses was a shepherd for his father-in-law, Jethro, who was a priest in Midian. And he led his flock to the most remote part of the wilderness where he came to God's mountain, Horev. And God's angel appeared to him in the heart of a flame within a **bush;** and he looked and thought the **bush** was on fire, but the **bush** was not being consumed by the fire. And Moses said, "I will turn and look at this surprising sight. Why won't the **bush** burn up?" And God saw that he'd turned to see what was happening, and so God called out to him from within the **bush.** And God said, "Moses, Moses." And he said, "Here am I."* (Exodus 3:1-4)

The sages say that there are five occurrences of the word *sneh* (bush) here, just as there are five occurrences of the word *or* (light) in the first paragraph about creation. This is a hint that the light Moses saw was a light that no other human being had ever seen: the light present at the very beginning of the universe. It's sort of like seeing the light from the Big Bang, from which the galaxies and stars were formed.

Now do you see what the phrase "hiding in plain sight" means? It's not hard to count these words and make these connections . . . you just have to slow down and really look.

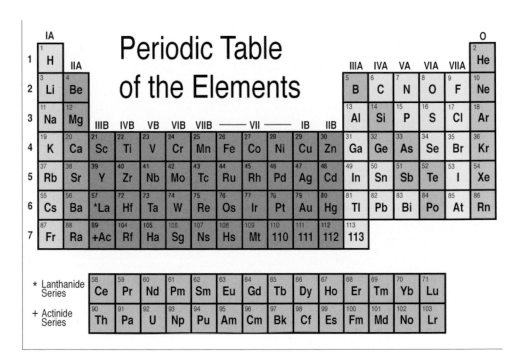

Periodic Table of the Elements

IA																	O
1 **H**	IIA											IIIA	IVA	VA	VIA	VIIA	2 **He**
3 **Li**	4 **Be**											5 **B**	6 **C**	7 **N**	8 **O**	9 **F**	10 **Ne**
11 **Na**	12 **Mg**	IIIB	IVB	VB	VIB	VIIB	——— VII ———			IB	IIB	13 **Al**	14 **Si**	15 **P**	16 **S**	17 **Cl**	18 **Ar**
19 **K**	20 **Ca**	21 **Sc**	22 **Ti**	23 **V**	24 **Cr**	25 **Mn**	26 **Fe**	27 **Co**	28 **Ni**	29 **Cu**	30 **Zn**	31 **Ga**	32 **Ge**	33 **As**	34 **Se**	35 **Br**	36 **Kr**
37 **Rb**	38 **Sr**	39 **Y**	40 **Zr**	41 **Nb**	42 **Mo**	43 **Tc**	44 **Ru**	45 **Rh**	46 **Pd**	47 **Ag**	48 **Cd**	49 **In**	50 **Sn**	51 **Sb**	52 **Te**	53 **I**	54 **Xe**
55 **Cs**	56 **Ba**	57 ***La**	72 **Hf**	73 **Ta**	74 **W**	75 **Re**	76 **Os**	77 **Ir**	78 **Pt**	79 **Au**	80 **Hg**	81 **Tl**	82 **Pb**	83 **Bi**	84 **Po**	85 **At**	86 **Rn**
87 **Fr**	88 **Ra**	89 **+Ac**	104 **Rf**	105 **Ha**	106 **Sg**	107 **Ns**	108 **Hs**	109 **Mt**	110 **110**	111 **111**	112 **112**	113 **113**					

* Lanthanide Series	58 **Ce**	59 **Pr**	60 **Nd**	61 **Pm**	62 **Sm**	63 **Eu**	64 **Gd**	65 **Tb**	66 **Dy**	67 **Ho**	68 **Er**	69 **Tm**	70 **Yb**	71 **Lu**
+ Actinide Series	90 **Th**	91 **Pa**	92 **U**	93 **Np**	94 **Pu**	95 **Am**	96 **Cm**	97 **Bk**	98 **Cf**	99 **Es**	100 **Fm**	101 **Md**	102 **No**	103 **Lr**

Finding Kabbalah Through The Hebrew Alphabet

*A*nother way to uncover the secret wisdom of kabbalah is through the Hebrew alphabet. This is called *gematria*, looking for hidden meanings in the numerical values of letters, words, or phrases.

This sort of kabbalah is a bit like chemistry.

This sort of kabbalah is a bit like chemistry. It is found in a book called *Sefer Yetzirah, A Book of Creation*. In chemistry, you learn about the elements and how they are organized by looking at the Periodic Table.

The location of the element, as well as its numerical value, help you to understand many of chemistry's mysteries. An enormous amount of information is packed into such tiny letters as H (Hydrogen) and O (Oxygen). When two H molecules combine with one O molecule they form H_2O—water.

So in this form of kabbalah, each letter represents a different kind of "element" in the world's creation.

Hebrew letters have the following numerical values:

א	*alef* - 1	י	*yod* - 10	+ אֶחָד = אַהֲבָה
ב	*bet* - 2	כ	*chof* - 20	
ג	*gimmel* - 3	ל	*lamed* - 30	
ד	*daled* - 4	מ	*mem* - 40	
ה	*hey* - 5	נ	*nun* - 50	
ו	*vav* - 6	ס	*samech* - 60	
ז	*zayin* -- 7	ע	*ayin* -- 70	
		ה + אֶחָד = אַהֲבָה		
ח	*chet* - 8			
ט	*tet* - 9			

One of the easiest numerological insights in gematria is this combination:

$$\text{יְהוָה} = \text{אֶחָד} + \text{אַהֲבָה}$$

Ahavah + Echad = Adonai
Love + One = God

The letters in the word love, *ahavah (alef, hey, bet, hey)* add up to 13 (1 + 5 + 2 + 5), and the letters in one, *echad (alef, chet, dalet)* also total 13 (1 + 8 + 4). If you combine the numerical value of the two words, you get 26, the value of God's name—*Adonai*—which is represented by the letters *yod, heh, vav, heh* (10 + 5 + 6 + 5 = 26). This exercise tells us that God is uniqueness and love combined.

Another important and easy example of this sort of numerology is God's first command to Abraham to leave his homeland and go to Israel. God's command in Hebrew is *"Lech l'cha"*—*"You shall go out."*

לֶךְ-לְךָ

The shapes and numerical values of these letters give us important messages. The letter *lamed* goes as high up as any Hebrew letter, while the final form of the letter *chaf* goes down the lowest. So one could interpret the command to be: "Use everything within you, from the top to the bottom, to make your journey."

In addition, *lamed* has a numerical value of 30 and *chaf* a value of 20. So the two words in this phrase have a numerical value of 100 (50 x 2). This denotes something utterly complete and perfect in our base-10 number system. Going on a spiritual journey takes everything we can give it, from our highest faculties to our lowest ones, and as a result of this effort we can come to a place of wondrous wholeness.

> The sages believed that the very shapes of the letters and the order of the alef-bet had deep meanings.

Another way to find secret wisdom in kabbalah is to look not at the words, but at the shapes of the letters. Here are examples:

Alef Bet means learn wisdom *(Alef Binah)*.   א ב

Gimmel Dalet means show kindness to the poor *(Gemol Dalim)*.   ג ד

Why is the foot of the *Gimmel* stretched toward the *Dalet*? Because it is fitting for the generous to seek out the poor. And why is the top of the *Dalet* stretched out toward the *Gimmel?* Because the poor must make themselves available to be helped. And why is the face of the *Dalet* turned away from the *Gimmel?* Because help must be given in secret to prevent embarrassment.

Hey, Vav, Zayin, CHet, Tet, Yod, CHaf, Lamed:

הוזחטיכל

This sequence teaches, "And if you give charity to the poor, the Holy One *(Hey, Vav)*, will sustain you *(Zayin)*, be gracious *(CHen)* unto you, show goodness *(meiTiv)* to you, give you a heritage *(Yerushah),* and bind a crown *(Keter)* on you *(L'cha)* in the world to come.

The open *Mem* and the closed (final) *Mem* denote open teaching *(Ma'amar)* and closed or secret teaching *(satuM)*.

מ ם

The bent *Nun* and the straight (final) *Nun* mean that the faithful *(Ne'eman)* if bent will ultimately be straightened.

נ ן

Samech, Ayin: support *(Semakh)* the poor *(Ani'yim).*

ע ס

The final *Pey* suggests a mouth that opens to speak gossip, while the regular *Pey* represents a mouth that is closed and does not speak gossip.

פ ף

A bent *TZadi* and a straight (final) *TZadi* suggest that the righteous *(TZaddik)* is bent in this world and will be straightened in the world to come.

צ ץ

Kuf stands for *Kadosh* (holy); *Resh* stands for *Rasha* (wicked).

ק ר

Why is the face of the *Kuf* turned away from the *Resh?* The Holy One *(haKadosh)* said, "I will not look at the wicked *(Rasha)*." And why is the crown of the *Kuf* turned toward the *Resh?* The Holy One says, "The one who repents will receive a crown *(Keter)* like Mine." And why is the foot of the *Kuf* disconnected? To show that one who repents can be brought into God's favor through this opening.

SHin stands for *SHeker* (a lie) and   ש ת
Taf for *emeT* (truth).

Why are the letters of the word *sheker (Shin, Kuf, Resh)* close together in the alphabet, while those of *emet (Alef, Mem, Taf)* are far apart? Lies are plentiful while truth is rare. And why does a lie *(sheker)* stand on one foot (the foot of the *kuf*), while truth has a brick-like foundation? Truth can stand but falsehood cannot. *(Babylonian Talmud Shabbat 104a)*

Where Can I Find Kabbalah
In The Prayer Book?

The Priestly Benediction

Probably the most powerful kabbalistic prayer in Jewish liturgy is something you hear during services on any Shabbat or holiday and on other occasions as well. This most ancient of prayers was recited by the priests in the Temple in Jerusalem, a place of great beauty and mystery.

יְבָרֶכְךָ **יהוה** וְיִשְׁמְרֶךָ ׃

יָאֵר יהוה **פָּנָיו אֵלֶיךָ** וִיחֻנֶּךָּ ׃

יִשָּׂא יהוה פָּנָיו **אֵלֶיךָ** וְיָשֵׂם לְךָ שָׁלוֹם ׃

*Y'varech'cha **Adonai** v'yishm'recha.*
*Ya'er **Adonai panav eleicha** vi'chuneka.*
*Yisa Adonai panav **elecha** v'yasem l'cha shalom.*

May God bless you and keep you.
May God's countenance shine upon you and grace you.
May God's countenance be with you and give you peace.

There is no prayer so poetically formed as this priestly benediction which comes from the Bible: (*Numbers 6:24-26*). It is constructed of 3, 5, and 7 Hebrew words in each respective verse. There are 15, 20, and 25 Hebrew letters in the verses. When arranged as a pyramid, the center words—both horizontally and vertically—contain the heart of the blessing itself: *Adonai panav elecha,* "God's face is towards you."

If you add up the number of letters in this benediction, you come out with the number 60. Mesopotamia had a base-60 number system which is why we have 60 seconds in a minute, 60 minutes in an hour, 360 degrees in a sphere, and why numbers such as 6 and 12 are so important (e.g., 12 people on a jury, 12 months in a year, *chai* [18] equals 6 x 3). This benediction, therefore, is complete, perfect, and whole in the base-60 number system.

The Kaddish

You can find another kind of mysticism in another part of the service you probably know quite well: the kaddish. This song of praise to God is a kind of *Heichalot* mysticism.

Heichalot means "halls." In this kind of kabbalah, the individual is searching for God and must go through six heavenly hallways to reach the seventh hall where God's footstool is situated. The journey is dangerous, and there are various angels who seek to block your path by trying to make you believe that they are God. If you fall for their schemes, you fail. It is analogous to playing a game on your computer. You have to build up points and make the correct moves and kill the bad guys to move to higher levels and win.

The prayers of this school of kabbalah often have a lot of *hitpa'eil* verbs all in a row, as the does the kaddish. For example:

Yitgadal, v'yitkadash (May God make God's own holy name great and may God make God's own holy name holy)

*Yitbarach v'yishtabach (*May God bless God's own holy name and may God praise God's own holy name)

> **The words serve as a way to approach God in a meditative state.**

Hitpa'el verbs are reflexive. It's like the difference between the verbs "washing" and "washing yourself." *Heichalot* kabbalah uses these verbs to maintain distance between us and God. These reflexive verbs teach us that we can't make God greater or holier. God alone can do this.

So anytime you hear a prayer with a lot of *"yit"s* or *"hit"s* in it, you should think of this sort of mysticism.

Heichalot kabbalah also expresses itself in prayers with long strings of synonyms. For example, the prayer that follows the *Shema* in the morning service, begins with the words, "True and enduring, correct and everlasting, right, and faithful. . . . "

When you read them in English, these synonyms can sound very boring. They're even boring in Hebrew if you take the words at face value. Here's the trick to making this sort of prayer interesting: forget the literal meaning of the words and understand the words as a sort of chant. The words serve as a way to approach God in a meditative state. Because this school of kabbalah sees God as very far away, each word, each synonym, is a step through those long hallways in the journey toward God.

What Are The Basic Kabbalistic Texts?

The Zohar

It's likely that when you ask someone about kabbalah, the first thing they tell you about are the ten *sefirot* of God. They might show you a diagram that looks like the one at left.

This diagram by Christopher Benton is the representation of the kabbalistic system of Moses de Leon, a Spanish philosopher who published his work, the *Zohar,* which means "Splendor," in the late 1200s. It represents the ten sefirot, or processes, within God.

Another analogy may help you understand this concept. It may be difficult to remember the exact moment when you realized your parents had a life—thoughts, desires, actions—that was unrelated to you. They loved you, but they were also thinking about work, money, gaining weight, losing hair, and about their own parents. Once you understood that you were part of a network of things that was important to your parents, you could figure out your place in the system and find ways to interact with other parts of it.

In the Zohar, Moses de Leon describes a network of ten major processes, called sefirot (singular—sefirah), going on within God.

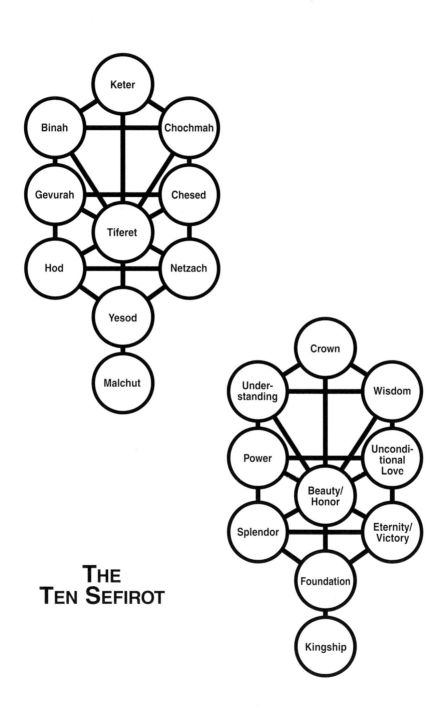

THE TEN SEFIROT

You have these same sefirot within yourself. Usually a person will have more activity going on in one or more of the sefirot than in the others. For example, if you are a person who loves wisdom and learning, your sefirot of *binah* (understanding) and *chochmah* (wisdom) may be more active than your sefirah of *hod* (splendor). If you are someone who loves to stay balanced, then you probably like to "live" in *tiferet* (beauty/honor) which moderates the opposition of *chesed* (unconditional love) and *gevurah* (power and suffering).

Each of the lower seven sefirot is associated with a different patriarch.

ABRAHAM,

who was kind to guests, represents *chesed,*
unconditional love.

ISAAC,

who had the terrifying experience of nearly
being sacrificed by his father, is linked with
gevurah, power and suffering.

JACOB,

who strove all his life to follow the middle path
that benefits both giver and receiver, created that
xquisite balance which the Zohar describes as
tiferet, beauty/honor.

41

AARON,

the first High Priest, wore the most beautiful robes
to perform Judaism's most solemn ceremonies, so
he is related to *hod,* splendor.

MOSES,

who brought us the Torah, which we can study
forever, is related to *netzach,* eternity and victory.

JOSEPH,

who led the Jewish people from starvation to a land
of plenty, is related to *yesod,* foundation.

KING DAVID,

the greatest king of Israel, is associated with the
lowest sefirah, *malchut,* kingship—which is how
we experience God here on earth.

Though these sefirot are in a hierarchy, it is only important right
now for you to know that you must not get "stuck" on *malchut*—
i.e., trying to understand God's actions in the world. If you are pre-
occupied with why it appears that some bad people have it good
and some good people have it bad, you'll never be able to
encounter the higher sefirot.

So: don't get stuck at *malchut!*

Finding the Zohar in the Torah Service

Now, remember what we said about much of kabbalah being
hidden in plain sight?

You probably already know about the sefirot. You just don't know
you do! Think about the Torah service. As the Torah is taken from
the ark and carried through the sanctuary, we sing the following
words from the Bible, first recited by King David:

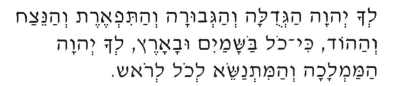

לְךָ יְהוָה הַגְּדֻלָּה וְהַגְּבוּרָה וְהַתִּפְאֶרֶת וְהַנֵּצַח
וְהַהוֹד, כִּי־כֹל בַּשָּׁמַיִם וּבָאָרֶץ, לְךָ יְהוָה
הַמַּמְלָכָה וְהַמִּתְנַשֵּׂא לְכֹל לְרֹאשׁ.

Yours, God, are (1) the greatness and (2) the strength and (3) the beauty and (4) the victory and (5) the splendor. (6) For everything that is in the sky and on the earth is Yours, God ,(7) for You have the kingship. (I Chronicles 29:11)

As we prepare to read from the Torah, we affirm that studying the Torah is a way to understand aspects of God.

When we sing this biblical verse during the Torah service, we are incorporating kabbalah into the ceremony. The qualities of God that David enumerates correspond to the sefirot:

1 *Gedulah = chesed*

2 *Gevurah = gevurah*

3 *Tiferet = tiferet*

4 *Hanetzach = netzach*

5 *Hahod = hod*

6 *Ki chol bashamayim uva'aretz = yesod*

7 *Lecha Adonai hamamlachah = malchut*

So as we prepare to read from the Torah, we affirm that studying the Torah is a way to understand these kabbalistic aspects of God.

4 3

And that's not all! There's actually a passage taken directly from the Zohar in the Torah service. Written in Aramaic, it begins with the words *"B'rich shmei d'marei alma,"* "Blessed be the name of the Master of the Universe."

You may be familiar with the end of the prayer that is sung before the Torah is taken from the ark.

בֵּהּ אֲנָא רָחֵיץ וְלִשְׁמֵהּ קַדִּישָׁא יַקִּירָא אֲנָא אֵמַר
תֻּשְׁבְּחָן. יְהֵא רַעֲוָא קֶדָמָךְ דְּתִפְתַּח לִבִּי בְּאוֹרַיְתָא,
וְתַשְׁלִים מִשְׁאֲלִין דְּלִבִּי וְלִבָּא דְכָל־עַמָּךְ יִשְׂרָאֵל,
לְטָב וּלְחַיִּין וְלִשְׁלָם. אָמֵן.

In the Zohar, this prayer is said in the context of describing the Torah service as a reenactment of the giving of the Torah on Mount Sinai. We should be as filled with awe when the ark is opened and the Torah is taken out as the Israelites were when the lightning and thunder accompanied God's giving the Torah to Moses. Here is part of what this prayer says in English.

You might already have begun your study of kabbalah without knowing it!

In God I put my trust, and to God's holy and glorious name I utter praises. May it be Your will to open my heart to Your Torah, and to fulfill the wishes of my heart and of the heart of all Your people Israel for happiness, life, and peace. Amen. (Zohar, Vayakhel 206a)

So now you not only know about the Zohar, you actually know a passage from it. You might already have begun your study of kabbalah without knowing it! And it's right there, in the prayer book, "hiding in plain sight."

Isaac Luria's Kabbalah

You also may have heard the phrase *tikkun olam,* which means "repairing the world." In kabbalah, this concept has even deeper meaning. The kabbalist Rabbi Isaac Luria (1510–1574), who lived in Tzefat, Israel, described God's "biography" so to speak.

44

According to this form of mysticism, God "contracted" into a place that the human mind cannot detect. This would be the same place that holds the light of the first day of creation, the light that Moses saw in the burning bush. This contraction is called *tzimtzum* in Hebrew.

God's light was meant to exist in this world, but the vessels that were to hold this light were not strong enough to conduct this energy. It's very similar to what happens when you have a short circuit.

An analogy: Let's say you were using your hair dryer when too many other appliances were running at the same time. The wires would overheat and trip the circuit breaker. That is similar to what happened to the universe when God's light came into it. The vessels that were meant to store the light couldn't handle the intensity of God's energy, and they shattered. This is called *sh'virat keilim,* "the shattering of the containers." Now, with the aid of human beings, God continues to work to repair the broken vessels. It may seem strange, but God needs our help to repair the world and its brokenness. In kabbalah, it is this repair work that is called *tikkun olam.*

Another analogy may help you understand *tzimtzum:* When you were a baby, your parents clothed you, bathed you, and fed you. As you grew, you became able to attend to more and more of these things yourself, so your parents stepped back and allowed you to take over choosing what you would wear and eat. As you grow more competent, your parents will continue to "contract" from your space, until you are a grown up and they treat you as an adult. It's almost as if they are going into exile from The Land of Parenthood. In Luria's version of God's "biography," God does what your parents do and "contracts" from the Universe.

But just as your parents leave within you the values they have taught you, the patterns of life that are probably so much a part of you that you don't question them, and, of course, their genetic legacy, so God's essence remains even after it contracts *(tzimtzum)*.

Another aspect of Luria's kabbalah is the idea that there are four worlds: (1) the physical world in which we live (Action/*Asiyah*), (2) the world of feelings (Formation/*Yetzirah*), (3) the world of the mind (Creation/*Briyah*), and (4) the world of the soul (Emanation/*Atzilut*). There are prayer books which uncover the meanings of these four worlds by manipulating Hebrew letters. It is a very advanced form of mystical meditation and should not be tried until one has mastered more basic kinds of prayer and meditation.

It may seem strange, but God needs our help to repair the world and its brokenness.

Why Is Kabbalah Kept So Secret And Why Do You Have To Be Ready To Learn It?

*K*abbalah is exciting because it allows you to reach an altered state of consciousness.

Because it can be a risky experience, it is kept secret. This is to keep you from going too far too quickly. You don't want to find yourself stranded in dangerous territory without a guide to help you or without the ability to help yourself.

This reminds me of something that happened when I was a child. My father bought me a really great kite and hooked it up to a fishing rod so I could let it go or reel it in as I wished. Once my kite flew and flew until it was just a speck in the sky. I began to reel the kite back in, but the wind was so strong and the kite so very high up that, try as I might, I could not get the kite back. Eventually, we had to cut the line and the kite sailed away out of sight.

You don't want to be like that kite and lose all connection with life on earth. You don't want to get so far up that you can't find a way back down.

> **We want you to "commute" to the upper spheres, not stay there.**

We want you to "commute" to the upper spheres, not stay there. Once you're married, have a job, friends, and ties to your community, you will always have a reason to come back to the realm of the everyday world.

Another reason to delay "doing" kabbalah is that kabbalah's insights can be frightening. When you finally realize that every single thing you do, every thought and feeling that you have, has an enormous impact on others, the world, and God, you may become paralyzed with fear lest your next action cause the world to fall. That's where the system of *mitzvot* comes in. It gives you good, ready-made ways to live your life in a way that helps you and helps the world.

What Does Kabbalah Teach About Astrology, Angels, Reincarnation, Karma, And Magic?

"*B*ut I thought Judaism doesn't believe in all those things!" I can almost hear you saying. I can assure you that it does. Kabbalah has all those things you thought belonged only to other religions—astrology, angels, reincarnation, karma, and magic.

Astrology

When you visit Israel, try to visit Kibbutz Beit Alpha in the Galilee. There you can see the mosaic floor of a synagogue that is 1500 years old. As you can see from the following pictures, the floor is divided into three sections.

THE FIRST SECTION IS A PICTURE OF THE BINDING OF ISAAC
(GENESIS 22:1-19).

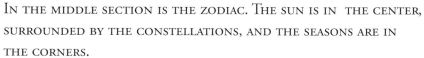

IN THE MIDDLE SECTION IS THE ZODIAC. THE SUN IS IN THE CENTER, SURROUNDED BY THE CONSTELLATIONS, AND THE SEASONS ARE IN THE CORNERS.

THE LAST SECTION CONTAINS SYMBOLS OF THE TEMPLE, SUCH AS THE
ETERNAL LIGHT AND THE ARK.

This beautiful mosaic floor takes you from the beginning of Judaism (Abraham), into the present (symbolized by the zodiac, which is a kind of calendar), and then into the future when the Temple will be rebuilt.

What's important to know is what we do with astrology in Judaism. We don't use it to predict the future or to gain power. We use it as a symbolic way of thinking about God's universe and celebrating our calendar as we move through the seasons.

By the way, this is not the only synagogue floor with a zodiac in it. There is another synagogue mosaic floor in Sepphoris in the lower Galilee which was discovered in 1993, that has everything included in this floor and more.

In Judaism, we don't use astrology to predict the future or gain power.

Angels

Starting with the Torah, kabbalah not only assumes that angels exist, but describes a variety of them. Some of them are enormous, and some are small enough to sit on the head of a pin.

In the mosaic of the binding of Isaac, which we mentioned above, the little hand coming down out of the sky to stop Abraham from sacrificing his son is the angel in that story.

In addition to archeological sources, we know about angels from the Tanach, Talmud, and the daily prayerbook. The Talmud says there are all kinds of angels—some who represent the different nations of the world, some who are God's helpers, and lesser angels and demons. (Yes, we have demons in Judaism, too.)

> In Judaism angels do not have one of the most precious things we humans have–free will.

The important thing to remember about angels in Judaism is that they do not have one of the most precious things we humans have—free will. This story from the Talmud shows the limitations of an angel's power.

Two ministering angels, a good one and an evil one, accompany each person home from the synagogue on Friday evening. If the candles are lit and there is a table cloth all laid out, and everything is ready to celebrate Shabbat, the good angel says: May it be this way next Shabbat, too. And the evil angel unwillingly says: Amen. But if no preparations for Shabbat have been made, the evil angel says: May it be this way next Shabbat, too. And the good angel unwillingly says: Amen. (Babylonian Talmud, Shabbat 119b)

Angels cannot act on their own. They can only respond to what human beings do. In this sense, angels have less power than human beings. That's why we don't ask angels for help in Judaism; we have more power than they do. Even the Zohar passage that we recite during the Torah service says, "Nor do I rely on angels." If we want help, we go straight to God and ask for it directly.

Reincarnation

Kabbalah teaches that there is reincarnation *(gilgul)* or, to put it more accurately, the passing of souls into successive bodily forms, either human, animal, or plant. A soul must return to earth until it has accomplished the mission it was given by God. Then it can stop coming back to earth and either stay with God or voluntarily return to earth to teach other souls the path to enlightenment.

How can a soul move from a woman to a tree to a dog and then to a man? Think of it this way. Fill a glass with water. We can all agree that the water is in the glass. Now break the glass.

The soul moving through different containers is very much like water moving through different vessels.

The water spills onto the floor, but it remains water. Next, wipe it up with a towel. Now there's no water on the floor because the water is in the towel. But it's still water. If you squeezed the towel over a new glass, you'd be able to fill it up with the original water. The soul moving through different containers is very much like this water moving through different vessels.

Here's another way to think about reincarnation. Who is president of the United States now? Who was president before, and who was the president before that? What each of the previous presidents did has a direct impact on what the current president has to do. The presidents before have either left a mess to clean up or a good situation that will permit the next president to move forward.

Additionally, once a president has served two terms, s/he cannot be president again. This is similar to reincarnation. The position stays. The occupant of the position changes. You, as you, are never going to appear again on this earth. So you must do what God needs you to do so that the next person in your position doesn't have to do his or her own work *and* your work.

So how do you know what God needs you to do? All you have to do is pray this prayer: "May it be Your will that I do Your will and that You let me know what You need me to do." Then watch and listen for the answer.

Karma

In Hebrew the concept of karma is called *middah k'neged middah*—"measure for measure." For example, we learn that the energy and feelings we send out determine the energy and feelings that will return to us:

The rabbis asked: "Who is honored? The one who honors others." *(Pirkei Avot 4:1)*

This teaches us that we must send out the energy that we would like returned to us. If you want honor, you should honor others. If you'd like friends, be friendly. If you want smiles, smile at others. And don't be surprised that when you send out anger, anger is what you will get back!

Are we merely pawns in a cosmic game of chess?

So do we control everything? Or are we merely pawns in a cosmic game of chess? As we said at the beginning, kabbalah teaches us to live with contradictions.

Rabbi Akiba gave us this puzzle when he said, "All is foreseen and free will is given." *(Pirkei Avot 3:19)*

I can see you scratching your head in puzzlement. Truthfully, I don't understand how this can be true, either. It's like the theory in physics that says an atom is a wave when you're not looking at it and a particle when you are. I don't get that one. So what do I do? I control what I can by sending out the energy I want back and then try to live tranquilly with what I cannot control.

There are many books about kabbalah that tell you how to make
amulets and magic formulas, but no
good teacher of kabbalah would
ever show these texts to you unless
s/he was absolutely certain that you
would read them only out of love for

> The real magic is not in trying to manipulate things. It's in seeing the beauty of things as they are.

learning and were not intending to misuse the magic.

The Talmud outlines the limits on who can know the 42-lettered name of God, which enables one to do magic:

The forty-two-lettered Name is entrusted only to one who is pious, meek, middle-aged, free from bad temper, sober and not insistent on his or her rights. And s/he who knows it, is heedful thereof, and observes it in purity, is beloved above and popular below, feared by people and inherits two worlds, this world and the future world. (Babylonian Talmud, Kiddushin 71a)

You can see why you have to have all these qualities in order to know this name of God. You can't use it in a fit of anger or if you're drunk. By the time you develop all these characteristics you'll have realized one of the most important truths of all: the real magic is not in trying to manipulate things. It's in seeing the beauty of things as they are.

What's With Those Red Strings?

R ed strings have a long history as amulets in Judaism and in other religions as well. The power of the red string is not just in tying one around your wrist.

The "classic" red string is one you get when you make a pilgrimage to Rachel's tomb in Bethlehem in Israel. The red strings given out there are usually accompanied with a prayer that one be able to become pregnant.

Unlike her sister Leah, who conceived and bore children easily, Rachel not only had a difficult time becoming pregnant but also died giving birth to her second child, Benjamin. She is buried in Bethlehem because that is where she died. Later, the prophet Jeremiah spoke of Rachel as forever weeping for her children as she waits by the road for them to return (Jeremiah 31:14). The red string reminds us of the sacrifice she gave, her very blood, to give life to her son. So the string represents sacrifice and life at the same time.

> The power of the red string is not just in tying one around your wrist.

You can also get a red string at the Western Wall in Jerusalem—for a donation. This red string will remind you of the beauty of Israel and the suffering our people have undergone, all the way back to Mother Rachel.

If you need physical reminders of God's presence, you can also put on *tefillin* or a wear a *tallit katan* with *tzitzit* under your clothing.

RACHEL'S TOMB, BETHLEHEM

How Can I Begin To Put All Of This To Use In Real Life?

Getting on the God Track

The incredible thing about you is your ability to "multi-task." You can be brushing your teeth, listening to music, reviewing for a test, thinking about a party, and feeling hungry—all at the same time. All you have to do is add a "God track" to this mix.

Talk to God all day long.

There are several ways to talk with God. One way is just saying what's in your heart, out loud. People won't think you're weird; they'll think you're talking on your cell phone.

Another way to talk with God is through the traditional prayers provided in the prayer book. The sages wanted us to be conscious of God all day long, so they gave us blessings to say. We're supposed to say 100 each day. For example:

When you open your eyes in the morning, you should say, *"Blessed be the One who opens the eyes of the blind."*

When you dress, you should say, *"Blessed be the One who clothes the naked."*

The goal is to be aware of God's gifts all the time. There are blessings for everything that you enjoy: food, housing, clothes, the glories of nature, and the miracles that happen—in your private life and in the world around you. I'm not going to give you the list of these blessings for the following reason: We tend to think that we have to say prescribed blessings and we have to say them in Hebrew. These blessings are good, of course, but for some they can get in the way of spontaneously connecting with God.

Just start with five "wows" a day and work up to 100.

Use your own words. Believe me, God understands English. It's perfectly fine to say, "Wow! Great sunrise, God!" or "Wow! Thanks for giving me great friends, God!" Just start with five "wows" a day and work up to 100. At that point, your "God track" will be up and running smoothly.

Another time-tested system of relating to God is by doing mitzvot (God's commandments). Lighting Shabbat candles or hearing the shofar on Rosh Hashanah is one category of mitzvah (between you and God). Another kind of mitzvah (between you and another person) would be visiting the sick, feeding the hungry, or helping the homeless.

You can do mitzvot to show others how pious you are, or because you want a reward from God for doing them. Naturally, those aren't the best reasons to do mitzvot. But you can also do them as a way of repairing the broken vessels of which Luria spoke. Do them to help make God whole again. Before they do mitzvot, kabbalists either think or say out loud that they are doing this mitzvah to unify God's name and God's being.

There is another way to add to your "God track." You can study Jewish texts, of which there is an endless supply. You can pick from

Torah or Talmud with any of their commentaries, or from the great Jewish philosophers or modern Jewish thinkers. There are libraries filled with nothing but books of Jewish learning, but even your public library has books on the Bible and Jewish history and philosophy. There are also plenty of places to learn online.

> Studying is God's way of talking to you, while praying is your way of talking to God.

Try to study a little something each day. Just open a Bible at random and read until something helps you connect with God. You don't have to read it in order. Psalms can be a good place to start. Think of it this way: studying is God's way of talking to you, while praying is your way of talking to God.

Living Righteously

Appreciating what God does is one way to put kabbalah to use in your daily life. Another way to make your life kabbalistic is by living righteously.

Here are six questions by which you can judge how righteously you are living. You have to be able to answer "yes" to these six questions.

1. Are you honest in business?

2. Do you fix times for learning?

3. Do you have children and/or students?

4. Do you act out of hope and not despair?

5. Do you add to wisdom?

6. Do you want to have a deep, personal, mystical relationship with God? (*Babylonian Talmud, Shabbat 31a*)

1. *Are you honest in business?*

The first question you must answer is not, "Did you keep kosher?" or "Did you light Shabbat candles?" In fact, none of the six questions is specifically Jewish, which makes sense when you realize that the journey to the very edge of existence, to the roof of the world, is the same quest for everyone. So the first thing that you have to work on is as simple, and as huge, as being honest in business. And this is not limited to working at a job.

You want to do business without hurting anyone. For example: according to Jewish law, if you are out shopping and don't have the money to buy something, you are not allowed to go into a store and ask the price of an item. To do that would be to waste the salesperson's time and raise his or her hopes of a sale. S/he might miss talking to a customer who really intends to buy something. And when you're tempted to use illegally downloaded music or movies, ask yourself if it's worth having this seemingly harmless crime on your spiritual record.

You have to be able to answer "yes" to these six questions.

2. *Do you fix times for learning?*

In our culture, we think of school as something we eventually leave behind us. In Judaism, you never stop learning. Even if you only set aside five minutes a day to read some Torah or even *The Jewish Encyclopedia* (online at www.jewishencyclopedia.com), you keep your mind open to the beauty of Jewish tradition. It's like setting aside time each day to exercise. On those days that you might not feel like exercising, you remember that the benefits—improved concentration, sleep, and health—are worth the discipline. And once you get started, whether it's studying or exercising, you usually feel better for having done it. There is a spiritual way of saying what you may have learned in science about inertia: "A body in motion tends to stay in motion, and a body at rest tends to stay at rest." The sages say it this way: One mitzvah begets another mitzvah and one sin begets another sin." (*Pirkei Avot 4:2*)

3. *Do you have children and/or students?*

In Judaism, a teacher is like a parent. This is nice because it means you can have an almost limitless number of "children" just by sharing what you know. Your knowledge might be about Judaism, or it might be about woodworking, calculus, physics, literature, or cooking.

> One mitzvah begets another mitzvah.

It can take courage to stick with what your soul tells you is your real area of expertise and what you should do, because it may not be what your parents think you should do, or what makes the most money. But if it's what you think God needs you to do, then doing it will bring you happiness and probably enough money to live on. By using your skills and knowledge, opportunities to teach will arise. In time, you may also have your own children who can benefit from your knowledge.

4. *Do you act out of hope and not despair?*

Acting out of despair or depression is forbidden in Judaism. Looking at Jewish history, you can see why this has been important. Many times in our history, our people have suffered and died, yet we did not give up hope. We have survived while great kingdoms that sought to kill us have died. This rule also applies on a personal level. Sometimes we can

> You're never too young to have brand new insights.

be overwhelmed with sadness: a relationship ends with a rocky break-up, friends betray us, we don't get the grades or make it into the clubs or teams we wanted to enter, our parents can't find a way to get along with each other, or friends fall seriously ill. It is difficult to stay hopeful in such situations. Judaism demands that you hold on to hope no matter how grim things appear.

5. *Do you add to wisdom?*

It's not enough to be a good student or to teach others. You have to add to wisdom so that there is more to be passed on to future generations. And don't think that you have to wait until you're older for this to happen. My children have taught me all kinds of new things. You're never too young to have brand new insights.

6. *Do you want to have a deep, personal relationship with God?*

The sixth question is, perhaps, the most personal. Only you and God can answer it. Do you meet with God in prayer, in study, in living a righteous life? Your relationship with God requires as much "maintenance" as any human relationship does. You have friends with whom everything is on the surface. Then you have friends with whom you develop a great sense of trust and caring. You can talk about anything with such friends, and they can confide in you, knowing you won't judge them or reject them. That's the sort of relationship God wants to have with you. You're that important.

By doing what it takes to answer "yes" to these six questions, you will be coming closer to God every day. It's as simple, and as difficult, as that.

By the way, the Talmud says that you will be asked these same six questions after you die. Your answers will determine your fate in the "World to Come."

How Can You Tell If A Teacher Of Kabbalah Is A Good One?

A good teacher of kabbalah will ask you many questions about yourself, your Jewish learning, your psychological state of mind, and your spiritual state of soul. A good kabbalah teacher will refer you to a counselor if you are having emotional problems rather than trying to treat those problems through kabbalah study. Even if the teacher feels you are a good candidate for learning kabbalah, s/he will begin slowly, searching to find out what you already know rather than giving you new information. Then you'll be taught one-on-one to make sure that you're not getting ahead of yourself.

> **Be wary of a teacher who wants to be needed and adored rather than having you need and adore God.**

Be wary of a kabbalah teacher who does not do a careful assessment of your needs and your physical and psychological states. Avoid a kabbalah teacher who asks you for lots of money and suggests that you buy things, even if you don't understand what you're buying or why you're buying them. Be wary of a teacher who wants to be needed and adored rather than having you need and adore God.

Let's return to our analogy of climbing Mount Everest. Who would you rather have as your guide: someone who lets his or her climbers take dangerous risks to make it to the top, so s/he can boast about it in a brochure, or a guide who would like you to reach the summit, but only if you can do it safely? A good guide will stop you and turn you around, even if you're only ¼ mile from the summit if s/he sees that you are growing weak and will not be able to make it back safely to your high camp. A good guide will not let your judgment be blinded by Summit Fever.

If all you want to do is learn about kabbalah and not actually practice it, then it's very easy to find books and classes that explain the nuts and bolts—and even more advanced ideas about the topic. Just realize that you are not really learning how to put kabbalah into practice in your own life.

It's something like a course I once took on Cosmology (a discipline within Physics which examines the nature of the universe). It was informally called Physics for Poets and it was simply wonderful. We learned all of this neat stuff about the universe, about black holes, and about the nature of the Big Bang . . . without once having to do any of the math that had yielded these insights! My learning was, naturally, superficial, but if I'd have had to do the math, I'd have been a dismal failure. Nonetheless, I enjoyed this peek into a topic that would otherwise have been closed to me.

Your Life Is So Much Larger
Than You Know

*O*ne of the reasons I became a rabbi was because of an experience that taught me how each of our lives is much larger than we know. I was working on an archeological dig in northern Ohio one summer while I was in college. We were digging up a Native American village. My "pit partner" and I were working in the burial area. (This was in the days before we realized this wasn't a respectful thing to do.)

As we worked, we found one patella (knee cap), then another . . . and then a third. We were truly puzzled, and it took a week of painstaking work to realize that we had uncovered two full-grown men buried one on top of the other: one laid out flat and the other curled up on his chest in the fetal position. I couldn't help but wonder what these two full-grown men had been to each other. Were they father and son, brothers, friends? And what had killed them at the same time? Had it been a hard winter? An epidemic? A war?

> God's plan for the universe and for us is so intricate and beautiful that there is no way we can see even a tiny fraction of it.

Then I realized the most astonishing thing of all. This grave was at least 500 years old. There was no way these men could have imagined me. And yet they were having an enormous impact on my life.

This made me realize that I had no real idea of how I fit into God's plan or how I could play a part in someone else's life long, long after I had died. God's plan for the universe, and for us, is so intricate and beautiful that there is no way we can see even a tiny fraction of it from our limited point of view. It made me want to work with God to create a world in which these connections could be made.

This insight helped me understand why some people's lives seem filled with sorrow for no identifiable reason and why others' lives seem filled with sunshine they don't seem to deserve. The answer is that it is often hard to see the big picture.

Look at the woven Torah cover at right. Imagine that you're a string in the cloth that makes up the dark letter *bet* at the top of the Torah cover. From your perspective, within the cloth, everything is dark. There is darkness to the sides, darkness behind, and darkness ahead. You might feel angry that your life is darkness, while for other letters, everything is light. You'd never be able to see, from within the fabric, that you are just as important, beautiful, and fortunate as all the light cloth around you.

The irony is that from God's perspective, you are an essential part of this tapestry. It's impossible to see things from God's point of view, but when things just don't seem right, remember how much greater your life is than you know. Let that knowledge bring you some peace.

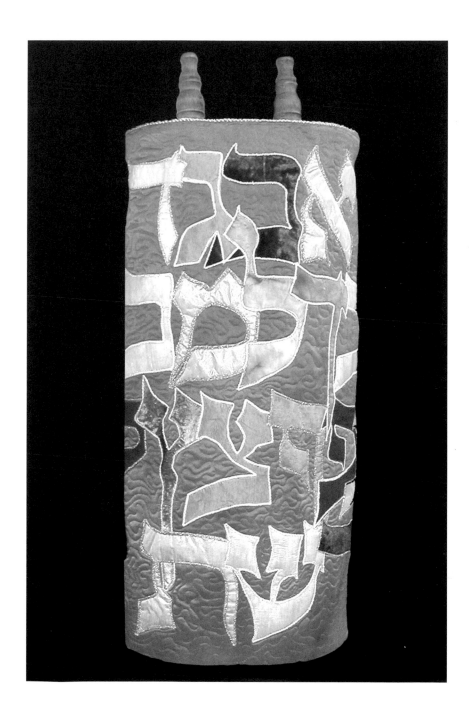

The words to this song sum it up nicely:

FROM A DISTANCE
By Julie Gold

From a distance,
The world looks blue and green
And the snow-capped mountains white.
From a distance,
The ocean meets the stream
And the eagle takes to flight.

From a distance,
There is harmony
And it echoes through the land.
It's the voice of hope,
It's the voice of peace,
It's the voice of every man.

From a distance,
We all have enough
And no one is in need.
There are no guns.
No bombs, no disease,
No hungry mouths to feed.

From a distance,
We are instruments
Marching in a common band.
Playing songs of hope,
Playing songs of peace,
They are the songs of every man.

Chorus

God is watching us
God is watching us
God is watching us
From a distance.

From a distance,
You look like my friend
Even though we are at war.
From a distance,
I cannot comprehend
What all this fighting's for.

From a distance,
There is harmony
And it echoes through the land.
It's the hope of hopes,
It's the love of loves,
It's the heart of every man.

Where Do I Go From Here?

*N*ow you know some of the basic information you need to decide whether you want to learn about kabbalah or learn to practice kabbalah. If it's the former, you'll find plenty of books available. If it's the latter, spend time preparing yourself for the journey. When you are ready, you will meet your guide. I wish you blessings on your way!

GLOSSARY

Gematria: Numerology. Each Hebrew letter has a numerical value. Hidden meanings are uncovered by comparing the numerical value of words and phrases.

Gilgul: Reincarnation. The moving of a soul from one body to another in successive lifetimes.

Heikhalot: Halls. This is the name for the kind of mysticism that envisions a journey through seven heavenly halls until one reaches God's presence.

Kabbalah: Hidden wisdom developed over many centuries through holy books and practices.

Ketuvim: Writings. The third major part of the Bible which includes the books Psalms, Proverbs, Job, Song of Songs, Ruth, Lamentations, Ecclesiastes, Esther, Daniel, Ezra, Nehemiah, I and II Chronicles.

Mitzvah *(plural mitzvot)*: Commandment. A major teaching and/or directive within Judaism. Mitzvot can concern the relationship of a person with God *(mitzvot bein adam laMakom)*, the relationship between people *(mitzvot bein adam l'chaveiro)* or between a person and his/her conscience *(mitzvot bein adam l'atsmo)*.

Nevi'im: Prophets. The second major part of the Bible which includes the books Joshua, Judges, I and II Samuel, I and II Kings, Isaiah, Jeremiah, Ezekiel, Hosea, Joel, Amos, Obadiah, Jonah, Micah, Nahum, Habakkuk, Zephaniah, Haggai, Zechariah, and Malachi.

Priest: In Hebrew *kohen* (plural *kohanim*). A hereditary class of persons entitled to offer the sacrifices in the Temple and to keep the Temple functioning. They, alone, were allowed inside the Temple building itself.

Sefirot *(singular sefirah)*: In the Zohar, the *sefirot* are defined as processes within God.

Shabbat: The weekly day of rest. It begins Friday evening at sundown and ends Saturday night after sundown.

Shofar: Ram's horn. It is blown most notably on the Jewish New Year.

Talmud: In this book, the term refers to the Babylonian Talmud, a great work of rabbinic literature, finished around the year 500 C.E.

Tanach: The Hebrew name for the Bible. An acronym of three Hebrew words: *Torah* (the first five books of the Bible), *Nevi'im* (Prophets, the books from Joshua to Malachi) and *Ketuvim* (Writings, the books from Psalms to II Chronicles).

Temple: The First and Second Temples (destroyed in 586 B.C.E. and 70 C.E., respectively) were located in Jerusalem and were the places wherein Jewish rituals such as animal sacrifices, offerings of incense, and the giving of the priestly benediction took place.

Tikkun Olam: Repairing the vessels that originally contained God's presence in the universe. The term is understood as repairing the world through acts of lovingkindness.

Torah: The word means "teaching" and is the name given to the first five books of the Bible: Genesis, Exodus, Leviticus, Numbers, and Deuteronomy.

Tzimtzum: The contraction of God's presence from creation.

Zohar *(splendor):* The title of a main book of kabbalah composed by the Spanish Jewish philosopher Moses de Leon around the late 1200s.

CREDITS

The images in this book were used with the permission of:

PhotoDisc (Illustration) Royalty Free by Getty Images, cover; © Laura Westlund/Independent Picture Service, pp. 13, 14, 25, 40, 74; © Todd Strand/Independent Picture Service, p. 28; © Chris Benton, p. 38; © Art Resource, NY, p. 50; © Erich Lessing/Art Resource, NY, pp. 51, 52; David Rubinger, Government Press Office, p. 60; Jeanette Kuvin Oren, p. 71.

From a Distance
Words and Music by Julie Gold
Copyright © 1986, 1987 Julie Gold Music (BMI) and Wing & Wheel Music (BMI)
Julie Gold Music Administered Worldwide by Irving Music, Inc.
International Copyright Secured. All Rights Reserved.

FOR FURTHER READING . . .

Blumenthal, David R. *Understanding Jewish Mysticism: A Source Reader*, two volumes (KTAV, 1978, 1982).

Idel, Moshe. *Kabbalah: New Perspectives.* (Yale University Press, 1988).

Liadi, Rabbi Schneur Zalman. *Likutei Amarim Tanya* (Kehot, 1993).

Matt, Daniel C. *The Zohar, Pritzker Edition,* several volumes (Stanford University Press, 2005, 2006).

Scholem, Gershom G. *Major Trends in Jewish Mysticism* (Schocken, 1941).

Swartz, Michael D. *Mystical Prayer in Ancient Judaism* (J.C.B. Mohr Tubingen, 1992).

Tishby, Isaiah. *The Wisdom of the Zohar*, three volumes (Littman Library of Jewish Civilization, 1994).

ABOUT THE AUTHOR

Rabbi Judith Z. Abrams is a woman with a mission: she wants to bring the beauty of Judaism to as many people, and with as much depth, as possible. She was ordained at the Hebrew Union College, earned her Ph.D. in Rabbinic literature from the Baltimore Hebrew University and is the founder and director of Maqom: A Place for the Spiritually Searching (www.maqom.com). She received the Covenant Award for outstanding performance in the field of Jewish Education and is a commissioned Senior Religious Advisor of the State of Texas. She lives in Houston with her husband and three children.